Get Christmased

Create the Christmas season that works for you and your family

Magda Pecsenye

CONTENTS

ACKNOWLEDGMENTS

Special thanks to Milo Razza, Kristina ElSayed, and Andrea Elias for their support and help in the creation of this workbook.

1 GET CHRISTMASED

Christmas (or Xmas, because the X is shorthand for the cross, or Christ) is the most hyped holiday in the world. Which means it's also the most confusing and painful holiday, especially since it's been stretched out from either 24 hours or 12 days (depending on your religious tradition) to more than a month.

Whether you believe that Christmas is a celebration of the birth of Jesus, a festive day for giving presents and spending time with family, a co-option of the solstice, a big consumer fraud, or just a day off work (or not!), you are probably overwhelmed sometimes with the whole season.

The Xmas season, for almost everyone, means PRESSURE:

- Pressure from your family
- Pressure from the consumerist culture
- Pressure to be appropriately religious
- Pressure from your past
- Pressure to create magic for your kids
- Pressure of wanting something but not knowing what you want

In this workbook we're going to:

- Uncover your ideas about Christmas
- Identify all the things about Christmas that can be problematic
- Discuss important concepts that might help you bring ease to your Christmas season
- Spend some time with the big unhappy elephants in the room--difficult people, depression, dissatisfaction
- Present some holidays that overlap with Xmas that might be of use to you
- Create a Christmas for your kids that is as great as the ones you had growing up, or better, or something (if you didn't do Christmas growing up)
- Identify what you want the Xmas season to feel like
- Make a plan for Christmas, including choosing meaningful (to YOU) themes and activities
- Write it all down in a master sheet to keep track of it

When we create your plan for what you want your Christmas season to be, we're going to pick themes that are important to you, and use those themes to determine what activities you're going to do. Without guilt.

By the end of this workbook, you will have explored and resolved (or decided not to think about, which is ok, too) your issues with and at Christmas, and will be ready to enjoy the season the way that feels best for your family.

This book is safe space.

There is no assumption in this book about you. No assumption that you're Christian or religious at all, atheist or Jewish or agnostic or Hindu or indifferent. And of course no assumption that you're any particular sex or gender or family configuration or ethnicity or nationality or anything. I am offering a lot of different options with the hope that you'll feel free to try things on and see if they feel meaningful or fun to you, even if they're not within the normal paradigm of what you do or believe. In other words, it's ok to try out Advent if you're not Christian unless it doesn't feel good to you. It's ok to discard whatever they told you in church about Christmas when you were five and do something else instead. It ok to sift through everything out there about Xmas and create a Frankenstein Xmas by stitching together something that makes the season meaningful, or at the least bearable.

Consider this your official invitation to come to a Christmas Eve midnight carol service whether or not you've ever been inside a church before, and especially if you're from a different faith tradition. Consider this your official permission to not go to church on Christmas Eve or Christmas Day if you're Christian. Consider this your permission to try on anything you're curious about or attracted to, even if it's not what you're "supposed" to be doing at Christmas.

A note about family and "family":

The religious and popular culture images of Christmas are of a heterosexual couple with children. The ultimate nuclear family. (Probably white, too.) Most of us don't fit that demographic, and even if we do, we're not perfect like the images of this ideal family are. (Can we talk about who buys a luxury SUV for their spouse--to appear in the driveway on Christmas morning--without talking about it together first?)

I'm going to talk about family in this book a lot. And what I mean by that is who you choose your family to be. Maybe it's you. Maybe it's you and your kids. Maybe it's you and a partner and a dog. Maybe it's you and your aunt. Maybe it's you and your two roommates. Maybe you actually are part of a couple and one or more children. (That's ok--you don't have to be media-perfect.) Maybe you have a large extended family that you're close to. Maybe you choose not to see all or part of your family because it's healthier for you. Be who you are and maintain your boundaries and include the family you want to include.

Let's start by jumping in and talking about what you think of when you think of Christmas.

Uncovering Your Ideas About Christmas

When I think of the word "Christmas" the ideas that come to mind are:

When I was little, Christmas was like:

Now that I'm an adult, Christmas is like:

What I love about Christmas is:

What I hate about Christmas is:

I feel stressed and guilty about:

I wish I could:

If there were three things I could change about the month of December, they would be:

Go back and look at the things you wrote down. What things gave you the most joy?

We're going to keep those things and try to expand on them.

What things gave you the most pain?

We're going to try to eliminate those things from your life during the Christmas season.

2 THE JUGGERNAUT

For most people, Christmas isn't just Christmas, because it's an entire season long. It's the entire month-long Christmas-through-New-Year-stretch. And for those of us in the United States, it's really the five-week stretch from the day before Thanksgiving through the New Year. That's a long juggernaut of managing expectations, dealing with family issues, spending money you may not have, and dealing with other people's emotions.

If you didn't grow up celebrating Christmas, don't celebrate it now, or celebrate other holidays such as Hanukkah or Solstice instead of or in addition to Christmas, it can feel like a long slog of being misunderstood constantly.

The rest of this book is going to focus on Christmas and making Christmas and the official Christmas season something you can stand, but I think it's important to take a minute to put it in context of the rest of this juggernaut.

Thanksgiving, New Year's Eve and New Year's Day, and any other holidays or milestones you celebrate in that time period can either work toward your peace of mind or against it. Only you know the best way to approach them to make things easier for yourself:

It might make things feel better for you if you have no plans for them at all and just let things happen. (But then you could get sucked into things you don't really want to do, like hosting people at your house for Thanksgiving or going to a party on NYE with people you don't like.)

It might make you feel more in control if you plan those days tightly and leave no room for anyone else to suck you into things you don't want. (But then you could be so focused on making sure the right things happen that you'll stress yourself out even more.)

It might make more sense to try to choose some sort of middle path in which you think about what your worst-case scenario for each other holiday or celebration is, and then do enough planning to make that impossible but still leave room for enough uncertainty that you don't get too focused on a rigidly-defined outcome of the celebration. But that means more planning, and thinking about what your priorities are for each holiday.

Thanksgiving: It's a day off for many of us, but not all of us. Is it about food for you? Spending time with family? Watching football? Prepping for sales (that might not be the biggest saving you'll find) the next morning? What would make it feel good for you?

The day after Thanksgiving: Do you shop on this day? Do you hide from the sales? Do you go out at midnight or before, or early in the morning? Does the whole thing make no sense to you? This day can be a big source of either fun or stress for people during this season. I'll recommend that you choose your stance and then stay out of the fray and don't put too much energy into conversations about it.

Hanukkah: A holiday that's simple and sweet on its own becomes fraught and high-stakes when it's forced into the same space as Christmas. Does it turn into an alternative to Christmas that makes it more important in the year of Jewish holidays than it actually is? Or does it maintain its low-key fun and get run over by Christmas so you have to dig in? It can be hard to find a balance if you have to contend with a lot of Christmas in your environment.

New Year's Eve: Prom for grown-ups, New Year's Eve seems to inspire fears of being socially excluded and never seems to be as much fun as you think it should be. So take that as you will. This night only has as much meaning as you give it. Choose deliberately to spend it in a way that makes you feel connected, even if that means spending it alone.

New Year's Day: You are not behind. No matter what you think you should have done already this many hours into the new year. And you can spend this day doing anything or nothing, with whoever you want to do anything or nothing with. It's not a predictor or condemnation of the rest of the year.

Birthdays falling in the long Christmas mega-season: If you place important on birthdays, it's important to celebrate birthdays falling inside the zone at least as much as you celebrate birthdays that fall during the rest of the year. People carry around hurt at having their birthdays ignored or undercelebrated for years, and all it takes to fix that is preparation. Plan birthdays--parties, gifts, other celebrations--before you plan anything about Christmas or the other holidays at this time of year. Buy presents first so they're more personal, and plan the celebration of the birthday as early as possible and send invitations so people have it on their calendars and won't be booked with Christmas stuff. If you get the birthday stuff taken care of so the birthday person feels good, the rest of the season will fall into place.

If you are responsible just for yourself, you can find a path through the season that feels ok. If you're responsible for others, either because they're your actual dependents or because people put their emotions onto you if you don't take charge, there's another layer of complication.

Managing family: Thanksgiving can make managing Christmas easier in some families and more difficult in others. If you're in a family in which locations need to be alternated (either because of divorce or just having multiple sides of the family), alternating Thanksgiving and Christmas can allow everyone to feel like they're getting something during the holiday. But if your main problem isn't dividing people up but spending too much time together. Thanksgiving PLUS Christmas all within one month (especially if people have to travel) can be excruciating.

You can opt out. You can stay home for one or the other (or both!) or go someplace else. (Yes, it's totally legitimate to go someplace else for Thanksgiving,, even if that involves not celebrating Thanksgiving.)

Or you can think strategically about which one is going to be less fraught and easier to live through, and then use that one to set up the other one for more ease. If Thanksgiving is traditionally a more relaxed day for you, then maybe it makes sense to invite your more controversial family members, so you don't have to see them on Christmas and make it even more fraught. (Or maybe you want to do the reverse so one holiday is like ripping off the band-aid and the other is truly free of tension.)

You can work NYE/NYD the same way, too, if you need to, by sacrificing one for the other. (Or celebrate both of them, or blow them both off.)

Note: It is entirely possible that you can't win. If your family operates in a way that puts pressure on your to solve things for them but then finds fault for the way you solved things, this is unfair and not something you can fix. If you can't escape this year, think about how you can minimize your contact and responsibility for things for the family. And think about how you can slip out from the yoke of everyone else's emotions for next year to be true to yourself. Even if they don't like it. They aren't going to like it even if you do everything perfectly, so stop playing a game you can't win.

3 ALMOST ALL THE THINGS THAT CAN BE PROBLEMATIC ABOUT THE CHRISTMAS SEASON

Here we are in the tough section of the workbook, uncovering stuff that can be stressful and painful about the Christmas season for you. There are a lot of things in this chapter. Some of them will apply to you, and some won't. If something doesn't have anything to do with you, just skip it. If something is important to you, work on it. If you can't face thinking about it right now, let it sit and come back to it in a few days when you've had some time to let it roll around in your brain and heart.

Be gentle with yourself. The whole point of this is to make some things obvious to you so you can get past them. Not to rub in hurts. If you need to back off, back off.

Before we go into this section, though, I want to say this: **There is nothing wrong with you.**

I mean, obviously you're not perfect, because no one is. But there isn't anything any more wrong with you than there is with anyone else. Nothing so broken or damaged that you can't be repaired to be stronger at the broken parts.

Repairing yourself at the broken parts is going to take deliberately shoving away the guilt so you can look at yourself with clear, loving eyes. And then being kind to yourself during the fixing process.

You're worth it.

Family Issues

This is huge during the Christmas season, even if your family hasn't ever celebrated together. The best-case scenario with families and the Christmas season is that you love your family but there are some things they do that annoy you. The worst-case scenarios seem to be a tie between loving your family but not being able to be with them (because of distance or death) and missing them horribly, and having been hurt by your family so much that it is not really safe for you to be with them but having to be there anyway.

Other bad scenarios include (but are not limited to): having to deal with multiple family obligations and being pulled in different directions and feeling like you're pleasing no one, feeling guilty because you aren't creating the same kind of fantastic holiday season for your kids that you had as a child in your family of origin, having no family you can trust and feeling alone, hating your family or in-laws, being excluded from gatherings or celebrations, feeling like your children are being hurt or slighted by family, and not being able to connect with family emotionally.

Your pain can be as simple as not wanting to sit through your Uncle Jerry's political rants at holiday meals or as complex as being forced to prioritize one side of your family over the other and having to fend off guilt and hurt feelings from multiple sides.

A lot of these family problems have common themes and repeating systems. The common themes that seem to cause us problems with our families are:

- guilt
- pain
- sadness
- loneliness
- alienation
- resentment

These seem to be problems with either things that you have that you don't want, or things that you don't have that you wish you had.

You can ease this by making some decisions about painful situations. Here are the steps to work through:

1. If it's something that you're asked to participate in that annoys you or makes you feel taken advantage of, see if you can come up with a solution that still achieves what your family wants but makes you feel good about your participation. If your family really wants everyone to be together and you've always come to your sister's house but you can't deal with that this year, maybe you can agree to have a different unit of people do the traveling vs. hosting and have it at your house instead (or a restaurant!). If you're feeling stressed about having to give presents to everyone (or to all the kids in the family, whether you have kids or not), maybe reconfigure who gives presents to whom so it's not uneven, or choose an activity to do together in lieu of giving individual presents. If family gatherings bring out competition and stress in certain pairs or groups of family members, consider having small events with individual people or small groups instead of one big gathering, so the people who compete never have to be together and competing.

If you feel consistent tension about the way Christmas happens in your family, it's likely that you're not the only one. So start putting out feelers to see if other family members feel the same way, and what you can do about it. If you feel consistent tension with another family member at Christmas, figure out if it's worth getting to the bottom of and working through (even if the first conversations are difficult), or if you can acknowledge that it's real and hurtful to you and then just move through it. (Sometimes other people just can't get past their own issues, so trying to "work things out" with them will get you nowhere and just cause more problems. If that's the case, then file that away under "Dropping Your End Of The Rope" and just try to limit interaction with that person, or control it so they feel validated but you haven't given anything up. There's more about this later on in the "Not-So-Shiny Things" chapter.)

Issues you want to address:

Issues you want to note for the (private) record but not address at this time:

2. If it's something you are asked to participate in that causes you pain, refuse as much as you can. Just because you've always done it doesn't mean you have to keep doing it. You can come up with an excuse, or just say you can't. Plan a trip somewhere. Get sick. Have transportation problems. But protect yourself and your kids and your pets and your partner (if you have them).

If you cannot get out of a hurtful family obligation, circle the wagons with your own little family. Talk ahead of time about how long the visit will be, what is likely to happen, what appropriate responses are, how long you will stay, what each of you should say as a code word to ask for help getting out of a nasty conversation. Prep your team to protect each other and stay together so you can get through a hurtful family obligation feeling supported and with as little damage as possible.

(Bonus: You're giving your kids the tools and the permission to protect their own boundaries in difficult situations and band together as a unit.)

Situations you want to avoid:

Situations you can't avoid but will manage carefully with your team:

3. If it's something you wish you had that you don't, see if you can recreate some of the feelings for yourself and your family in some other way. If you're missing people who are dead, you can share memories, cook their favorite foods, and otherwise surround yourself with things that remind you of them. If you're missing people who are still around but not physically near you, do Christmas by Skype or phone, so you can be together even if you're not physically together. If you're missing a family you never had or parenting you never had, create your own family with friends and parent yourself the way you wish you'd been parented.

You get to choose to have what you want.

What do you want to create, family-wise, that you don't have?

Kids (Read both sections!)

If you don't have kids:

Christmas is a really, really kid-centric holiday. Everywhere. The only exception, maybe, is the Dean Martin Christmas album, but everywhere else it's all kids and the "joy of family" and looking at a child's face on Christmas morning.

It can be a little hard to take if you don't have children. (Especially if you wish you did have children.)

And often, people without children get the short end of the stick in family celebrations of Christmas. If there's any traveling to be done, it's often on the childfree people, since it's logistically easier for them to travel in the big picture. That doesn't feel very fair, though, if it happens all the time. And then there's the gift-giving situation, in which childfree people give gifts to all the nieces and nephews AND the other adults, and only receive one present from the family unit. Yes, you are happy to give your nieces and nephews gifts, but the uneven financial burden seems extreme.

Even thinking about this stuff can make you feel Scroogey or cheap or resentful, and then you feel guilty about that. But it all chafes.

You have a right to be annoyed or angry about this. Give yourself 10 seconds or 10 minutes or 10 days to fume about it. Then come back and we'll work through it.

Back? Let's go.

You may be a person who likes kids, or you may be a person who doesn't like kids. (I'm in the second category. I'm a parenting writer who doesn't usually like other people's kids. I'm lucky that I like my own kids, but other people's kids notsomuch.) So you may find the hijinx of the kids surrounding you at Xmas to be entertaining, or you may find the kids to be unpredictable, loud, sticky, scary little creatures. But here's the rub: Those kids are going to be adults at some point. At some point in the future, that kid is going to be 25, and the two of you will be sitting on someone's sofa on Christmas afternoon drinking whiskey sours and talking about real stuff.

If you can connect to the actual person inside the kid, it will be easier for you to enjoy your time with that kid and not feel used.

A separate issue: The child's parents might be taking advantage of you either because they're selfish or because they're stressed and just aren't noticing that they're taking advantage. That is something completely separate from the children themselves. You can choose to say something to the parents to try to work things out or not, but that's a separate thing from how you interact with the kids.

For little little kids (under four years old), it's hard to have a real conversation, and you probably either find them cute or gooey and incomprehensible. But once a kid is school age, that kid has interests and knowledge. That kid is also way realer than any of the adults in the room, and if you're interested in a genuine connection, you can have it with the kid. Kids do know that they have to put on their game faces when they're with a bunch of adults, but if you talk to them on a person to person level and ask the kinds of questions you'd ask someone you wanted to get past small talk level with, you can have some great conversations. Some questions that can get you in are:

- What are you reading right now?
- What gift are/were you hoping to get this year?
- Do you collect anything?
- What's your favorite part about your favorite video game?
- Who did you go as for Halloween? Why?

You could also take this further and also solve the whole inequitable gifts aspect by having your gift to the child actually be an experience with you. Going to the art museum or zoo or a sports event or nature walk or pedicure, or anything that's at the intersection of something you're both interested in. It does not at all have to be expensive. (Depending on age, kids often have zero concept of financial value anyway, which is why they ask for ponies for their birthdays.)

Working on the connection with the actual kid will only improve with time, as kids get more interesting as they get older and are more interested in you. And they're the future of your family, so actually knowing them helps keep your family happy and harmonious instead of disconnected and resentful.

But what if you genuinely don't like a child? Well, kids are people, and you don't have to like all people, so that's normal. Just make sure that your dislike is actually based on the child and not on how the child's parents make you feel. They're two separate issues.

Now, having said all that, if you really can't stand to be around the kids, either because you're in pain from not having your own kids (especially if you're in the middle of infertility or going through a miscarriage or other loss) or because you just feel too irritated around them, excuse yourself. Make other plans and do something else for the time you'd normally be required to be around the kids. You can tell the truth or make up a story. Go away on a trip or just hole up in your house eating gingerbread. If you need to protect yourself, protect yourself.

If you don't need to protect yourself, though, try to connect with the actual people inside the kids' bodies.

If you have kids:

The amount of trauma having kids causes during the Christmas season is vastly underestimated. The whole "Christmas magic through the eyes of a child" angle is covered completely by every single bit of media, but there are all kinds of ways we are hurt by the experience of having kids that we don't talk about. Everything from not having enough money for presents and activities, to being limited in the celebrations we can have and the decorations we can put up because of the kids, to being lonely because we're at home with sleeping children instead of with friends, to feeling like we're failing them, to feeling like we just don't know what we're doing, to resenting the mess, to secretly thinking we shouldn't have had children in the first place.

It is completely 100% ok to be having any combination of those feelings.

Yes, I know you are lucky to have kids (so am I), but it's not a purely positive experience all of the time, and it's healthy to admit that. Don't give in to the temptation to play Misery Poker by comparing who has a worse situation. If you feel bad about something, you feel bad. It doesn't diminish anyone else's pain to acknowledge your own.

If you are feeling like you're failing your children by not creating for them the kind of ideal Christmas you'd like them to have, there's an entire section of this workbook about exactly that, toward the back of the workbook.

If you feel like you're failing your kids in general, let's take a look at that.

I do NOT think you're failing your kids, fwiw. (If you came to this workbook without knowing my website, AskMoxie.org, I've been writing parenting advice for ten years, and have seen a lot of parenting, and I think you're doing a great job.)

Here's the process I use for myself and for other people when we're figuring out what's going wrong and how to fix it:

1. Identify what you think is wrong. Write it down, as simply but completely as possible.

2. Now take a look at it again and think about what's happening from the other person's point of view (if there's another person involved).

3. Using both of those narratives (because the truth lies somewhere in between, probably), circle the problem points. The bottlenecks, or wrong decisions, or places where someone's reacting out of fear instead of love, or where there aren't enough resources.

4. Figure out what you can do to fix those problem points. You might need to revise your routine, or get help from another person (either the person involved in the situation or an outside person), or build some skills you don't have yet, but you can figure it out.

5. Remember that this is not a zero-sum game. If you're trying to improve something that's happening involving another person

(especially your kid), you both win together. So don't be afraid to be creative, or to try things to see if they work, and then switch it around if it doesn't.

Do that five-step method for any issues you have surrounding your kids. See if you can improve the process, because it's not about you being a good or bad parent, it's just about whether or not your process can be improved.

Then, cut yourself some slack. Especially during the Christmas season, when things seem more high stakes, when there are postings about perfect families and perfect parents everywhere, when it's easier to feel like you're the only one who doesn't have things together.

If you are feeling like you shouldn't have become a parent at all, try to identify if that feeling is coming from feeling like you just don't have enough (time, energy, emotion) right now, or if this stage is so difficult that you just can't see how it's possibly worth it (if your child is 18 months, 3.5 years, 4.5 years, 6.5 years, 7 years, or 9 years, you have my sympathies), or if you truly don't think you should have become a parent.

If you don't have the resources right now, can you ask for help? Your friends and family love you, and will want to help you if they can. Babysitting, inviting you over for dinner, or even just letting you vent or troubleshoot are ways your friends can help you get a little breathing room right now.

Most parents have at least one stage of human development that they don't enjoy. There is nothing wrong with finding more negative than positive in any particular age of your child. Know that if any specific age or stage is defeating you, all you have to do is keep waking up in the morning and in a few months your child will be acting differently.

If you think that, independently of any other challenges you have right now and independent of any age your child is right now, you should not have become a parent, that is real and serious, and you owe it to yourself to find a professional you can talk to to both validate your feelings and help you come up with a plan to help you come through this. You are NOT the only one and it doesn't make you a bad person at all.

Parenting is hard. You can do it.

Burdens of past Christmases

What if you have so much baggage left over from your childhood Christmases that you can't think clearly about Christmas?

You can always skip Christmas entirely, if you want to. Go on a trip somewhere, or just stay home and watch movies all day.

If you want to celebrate Christmas, though, you might have success if you make a plan to celebrate in such a radically different way than you have in the past that it doesn't trip the same wires in your brain. For example, if your childhood Christmases involved a lot of relatives, stiff fancy clothes, and too much sitting around being criticized, specifically plan a Christmas that includes solitude or only one or two people, comfortable clothes, and a lot of physical activity. Or go out for Chinese food and a movie. Volunteer at a homeless shelter. Volunteer to work shifts for co-workers who do want to be with their families. Doing something totally different allows you to break the associations you had and gives you control over your own experience of Christmas.

You can't afford it

Whether it's just Christmas you're worried about affording, or you're having 3 am insomnia from general money worries, you are not alone. Worrying about money is extremely stressful and makes you feel trapped.

Do not spend any money you can't easily spend on Christmas. Just don't. You don't need to travel. You don't have to give big gifts. You don't have to have big meals. Your family and children will understand that you can't afford things this year.

There is no shame in being short on cash in a difficult economy. And there's a lot of dignity in spending only what you really can on Christmas.

It's a better use of your brain power to think of ways to improve your financial position over the next year than it is to worry about having a Christmas celebration you can't afford this year. You can do this.

You're faking it

Maybe you're feeling pressure to make everything perfect. Maybe you don't think you're good enough. Maybe you're faking it. Maybe you feel trapped. Maybe you have no friends you can trust.

Stop looking at the school moms with the perfect lives. Close Pinterest, and read Facebook with a grain of salt. You know how to pose those exact same pictures to post on IG, so don't assume those are true for other people any more than they are for you. Make an effort to focus on the friends who really know you. Who really like YOU, as you are, and not the face you present to the world. Friends you allow to come over even if your house isn't clean. Focus on your relationships with them instead.

And if you don't have friends you can be completely honest with, no wonder you're feeling pressure to fake it. You're basically isolated from true relationships that are based on who you really are, and that's lonely. It hurts a lot.

Think about the people you know right now and determine if any of them could be friends you could really trust with yourself. If there are any of these people, try it out by exposing some of yourself to see how they respond. You could end up with real friends from this.

If no one from your current group will understand the real you, think about what qualities you're looking for in friends, and then start keeping your eyes and ears open for those people. Maybe there's someone you already know but have never really interacted with at work or your gym or your kids' daycare or school, or some other activity you do. The right people are out there, and you will find them once you're not afraid to step off the faking it treadmill anymore.

Reaching out can be scary and hard, but the more you do it the easier it gets. Not everyone will like you, but the right people will. It's worth the occasional rejection to get to good friends. Keep going.

Your marriage has problems

Christmas can be the worst time of year if your marriage is having problems, because all the family expectations and love mythology is in full force. Everyone thinks that you're fine because you're married, but if things aren't good it's lonelier and more alienating than being alone. (I've been both, and unhappily married is way more alienating at the holidays than being alone is.)

If you can let go of your own personal expectations for a sparkly, family Christmas and use the season for quiet contemplation about your situation and what you want to do about it, you can have a useful--if not happy--Christmas season. Nothing is going to make you happy right now anyway, so use this time to think calmly about what you want. Where do you see yourself next year? When you think about a year from now, which fills you with dread--the though of being in your same marriage or the thought of being out of it?

I think we know in our hearts what we need before we know in our brains. So allow yourself to just sit with it for awhile and to listen to what you already know about what you want next.

You can do this, whatever it is.

For further reading: *Getting The Love You Want* by Harville Hendrix and *Uncoupling* by Diane Vaughan.

Divorce

Divorce is a new beginning, and gives you the chance for real satisfaction with your life. But it can be rough during the Christmas season on a lot of fronts. If you're in the middle of it or new to the whole decision, this season can be agonizing, especially if you haven't told many people yet. Even if you're a year or two out, if you aren't embedded in a group of friends you love or in a new relationship yet you can feel lonely during this season. Here are my tips for making it through the Christmas season during divorce, originally published at http://askmoxie.org/blog/2012/12/divorce-2012-holiday-edition.html:

Divorce, Holiday Edition

Once upon a time, I told my then-husband I wanted a divorce a few days after Thanksgiving. That first December was hard. This is what I've learned since then about the first post-split holiday season, and offer it to you.

1. Let yourself be sad. This time of year is chock full of bullshit about being filled with the wonder of the season at every second. You're allowed to be sad, and you have a reason to be sad. Maybe you didn't like this time of year anyway, even before the divorce happened. Maybe you always liked it before. If you liked it before, you'll like it again. Just not this year. This year sucks, and it's ok to be sad. You're feeling just what you need to be feeling right now.

2. Look realistically at what you feel like your kids are missing. If this is the first year without their parents together for the holidays, your kids are going to feel sad, and they're going to feel like something's missing. (No matter how many toys you buy them.) That's normal and ok. Next year will be better for them, because by then it will be regular and not scary to be with each parent separately. But this year they'll need extra hugs. This is the part that hurts in order to feel better.

3. Think about what kind of family you want to be this time next year. This year is tough because you're feeling the sting of not being the family you (thought you) were before. But next year at this time you'll be a new family, one that's honest and loving and true. Spend some time thinking about what you want next December to look like with your new improved family, and what you can do to get there over the next year.

4. Think about what you're really missing. Are you missing the actual relationship? Being in a relationship in general? Or the Holiday Fantasy Relationship? You might actually be feeling great not to be with your soon-to-be-ex, but it still hurts that no one's going to surprise you with a car with a big red bow on it. Figure out exactly

what you're missing, and let the parts you're not missing drift out of your mind. And see if you can't get some of the stuff you are missing from family and friends.

5. Consider wallowing. Especially if you haven't let yourself wallow yet, now might be the time.

5a. I made you a playlist: spoti.fi/WcrOoQ

6. Accept. Accept help. Accept invitations. Accept hugs. There are a lot of people who love you. Let yourself be around them, even if you feel like crappy company. Brush your teeth and put on a clean shirt and go when someone calls you. Let people be your friends.

7. Know that next year will be better. I know, it's awfully Pollyanna-ish to say. But it's true. Everyone said the first year was hard but the second year was easier. And they were right. The third year is even easier. And by the fourth year this will just be a faded Rothko painting in your memories. Except that you'll be stronger and better and deeper and softer where it matters.

You can do this. Courage.

If part of your pain at the divorce involves not having had children and wanting them, and you're comparing yourself in the middle of the divorce to families that are together at Xmas, don't. Please don't. The Christmas season is a time when families can put on a happy shiny face, but you have no idea what's happening inside the family. So it's really not fair to yourself to compare the brutal, failing-feeling you to the shiny perfect-looking family you see. It's a false comparison. And it hurts you. And you don't deserve that hurt.

Being divorced with kids during the Christmas season can be tricky and hurtful, too, although many people find it easier to navigate the definite boundaries of divorce than to try to parent with their children's other parent when the relationship is not in good shape. Things will be easier when you come up with definite plans for gifts, activities, and Christmas Day.

Here are some topics if you're divorced/divorcing during Christmas and have kids:

Gifts: Some co-parents coordinate gifts for kids and decide who will give what and possibly even collaborate on larger items. Others specifically do not coordinate. Either method seems to work out, as long as everyone knows what's happening ahead of time.

Activities: Will both parents attend all activities (church or school programs and performances and other activities)? If there are new partners in the picture, will they attend? What about extended family from both sides? Even if you can't agree and end up resorting to rock-paper-scissors to decide who attends what, make a decision so there's less chance fighting at the event and so your child doesn't feel responsible for refereeing.

Christmas Day: There are three ways that seem to be successful for co-parents who choose one of them. One is to completely isolate the holiday, so one parent gets all of Christmas Day or longer (a set period of days surrounding it) and the other gets the children alone at another time. Another is to split the day so one parent gets one half and the other gets the other half (a variant of this is giving one parent Christmas Eve and the other Christmas Day). The third is for the co-parents to commit to spending Christmas Day together with the children. One of those probably made you cringe. Another one probably made you think, "I guess I could do that." Pick the one that feels least stressful and gives the most space for finding joy with your children on the day.

As long as you and your co-parent can agree and stick to the boundaries you establish, it doesn't matter what other people think. Your family may not understand why your kids can't be there for a given event, or may need reminding that they can't bad-mouth your child's other parent in front of your child. Or that they can't bad-mouth YOU for not being in a quote-unquote perfect family anymore. It gets easier as more time passes and everyone becomes more comfortable with the arrangement. Divorce gives people a chance to be who they really are and be happy with who they really are, and often that spreads to your extended families.

If you won't be with your kids on Christmas and you're having a hard time with this, remember that one day doesn't make or break your relationship with them. Kids are more likely to remember the small moments with you than any one specific day. So focus on all the other time that you spend with them so that the missing them today will be manageable sadness, not an emotional crisis.

Loneliness

A lot of us are lonely during the Christmas Season. Even people who look like they have perfect, connected lives. The only cure for loneliness is making genuine connection with another person. Someone has to do it. Take the chance, and push yourself a little, and you could win big. (You're worth it.)

You're depressed

If you have been managing your depression, keep at it. Keep taking your meds, seeing your therapist, accepting help from friends, going out into the sunshine every day, sleeping when you can, eating when you can. Allow yourself to take advantage of some of the stillness of the Christmas season without expectation of yourself.

If the depression is new, or you haven't been managing it, reach out. Tell someone--a friend, your doctor. You can get help managing it so you can function and feel good again. Managing depression doesn't have to include meds, and meds help a lot of people. You can feel better.

You were abused and you have to see those people

To you:

If you are expected to go to an event with a person who abused you, who knew about abuse and denies it, or who failed to protect you in any way, you do not need to see them.

All you have to say is, "I can't come this year."

It doesn't matter if other people want you to come. You have the right not to be around people who hurt you. Especially at Christmas.

I am giving you permission right now and for the rest of your life to protect yourself and to opt out of any and all events including people who have hurt you.

You are worth protecting.

Be gentle with yourself.

Food

This time of year is killer for people trying to manage food issues, whether it's allergies and sensitivities or eating for health or weight loss.

Do the best you can.

If you're eating for health or weight loss, make a plan for how you'll decide what to eat and what not to eat (plans could include: stick strictly to your plan, free-for-all, selected off-plan eating, some other system) and then do that. If you miss one day, just get back onto your holiday plan the next.

If you're managing allergies, find a couple of recipes you can always eat that feel holiday-indulgent, and bring those along whenever you go to an event. And let people know what you or your kids can't eat and what you can instead. You are not the only people with allergies, and most people are happy to provide safe foods if they know what they are.

It's ok to be annoyed/anxious/exhausted about food issues, especially at this time of year. You're doing a great job.

You have a chronic illness

Do what you can do. Don't push yourself just because it's the Christmas season or because people have expectations of you based on incomplete understanding of your illness. Find the things that bring you joy, and do what you can do of those things.

One great thing about the Christmas season is that the people who don't get it are often busy with other things and leave you alone. The downside is that your friends who do get it are often busy with other things so you don't have as much contact with them as usual. It's even more important to put together your own support group of other people dealing with chronic illnesses.

Anxiety and Panic Attacks

If there is something that comes up a lot around the Christmas season that causes you anxiety or panic attacks, be kind to yourself. There are all kinds of things that you're really good at, so the things that cause you anxiety are not that important. Everyone has things that make them anxious. And plenty of us have panic attacks. It doesn't mean there's anything wrong with you. It just means you're overloaded and this isn't the best situation for you.

There's all sorts of advice about permanently overcoming anxiety and panic attacks, but I think that's something to work on during the other 11 months of the year. During the Christmas season, when things are amped up and more stressful anyway, just be good to yourself, and try to think ahead to situations that will cause you anxiety. Then, either avoid them entirely, or get help managing the situations.

Sometimes, because a situation causes you anxiety, the importance of the situation becomes inflated in your head and it doesn't occur to you that you don't actually have to do it. Examples of that include: going into crowded shopping situations (like church bazaars, the mall, special Christmas markets, the grocery store the day before Thanksgiving), parties, singing solos in a choir performance (it's no shame to decline), and driving on long car trips.

Think about whether you really really need to do something that's causing you anxiety, or if you could just avoid it. Could you send someone else to take your kids to see Santa at the mall? (The kids remember seeing Santa, not who brought them.) Could you do your shopping in the middle of the night while the store is empty or shop online or hire a teenager to fight the grocery store for you? Would someone else be willing to pick you up and drive you someplace?

In situations you absolutely can't avoid, like your office holiday party or visiting your parents, you can enlist help to manage the situation so you aren't triggered. A friend at work can help block for you so you can get credit for showing up but you don't have to circle and talk to everyone. (Ask someone who loves to work the room, not someone else who hates parties. People who love parties are very happy to block for people who don't.) If visiting certain people makes you anxious, ask your partner (if you have one) to help you or bring along a friend (you can bring a friend along!) to help you manage the situation. Or be that rude jerk who's texting constantly with someone who's committed to being on call to text you through the event.

Whatever you do, don't force yourself to white-knuckle through it and berate yourself for being anxious in the first place. Seriously, EVERYONE has something that freaks them out. And you have a lot of amazing qualities you're just not concentrating on when you berate yourself for the anxiety. Treat yourself like you would your best friend, and cut yourself some slack.

You're addicted

If you're addicted to something, Christmas can make you feel like the fakest fake in the world. You may still be holding it together. Or maybe you think you're holding it together but other people can tell and you're avoiding them. Or maybe you're right on the edge.

You can get help. Now. Text or call your best friend or your mom or your sister or anyone whose number is in your phone. Say this: "I have to tell you something and I need your help. I'm addicted to [whatever you're addicted to] and I can't stop. I need help."

Job stress

If your job is stressful or unfulfilling or underpaid or hurtful in some other way, hang in there. I am absolutely not going to tell you that you're lucky to have your job and you should just try harder, because neither of those things is true. I am, however, going to tell you to use the Christmas season, with its cover of holiday shenanigans chaos, to really look at your job, figure out what you don't like about it, and make some decisions.

If something about your job changed (your pay, position, department, who you work with), would you be happy in it?

Is there something that would make staying in your job worth it (paid tuition, other training, the title, flexible schedule)?

Can you ask for those things? You might get them if you ask. If there isn't anything that would make staying in your job good for you, then you have to leave it. Think very carefully about exactly what you need in order to be happy in a work situation, and then only pursue those other jobs that have those things. It does you no good to get out of one job you hate and into another job with equal problems (exception: same problems but a much higher wage or flexible schedule).

Think strategically. Ask around (carefully). Use the Christmas season, when you'll be seeing people you don't see often and meeting new people, to let people know you're looking for something new. You don't have to say you hate your current job; say you're ready for more challenge and responsibility. Ask people to ask around and to keep you in mind. (More job connections are made through casual friends and acquaintances than through close friends. There are actual research studies about this. Close friends already know you're looking so they'd have recommended you already if they could. And casual friends and acquaintances know more people you don't already know, so they cast a wider net for you. Chat with people you don't know and ask for leads.)

It is depressing to be stuck in a job you hate at Christmas, but you don't have to be stuck. Use this time to set yourself up to find something new right away in the new year.

Cultural promotion of Christmas

The cultural promotion of Christmas as the Ultimate Experience can be unnerving to all kinds of people. Christians who celebrate Christmas as the birth of Jesus can be offended (especially since Christmas isn't even the most important Christian holiday), as can those of other faiths and agnostics and atheists who either celebrate culturally or don't celebrate Christmas at all. It causes an incredible amount of hurt and frustration considering how cheerful it pretends to be. People who try to push back against it seem to be more frustrated than before they started pushing back, so here are some ways to get through the season without losing it because of all the commercialism and hype:

Unplug. If you turn off mainstream media and don't go out into stores a lot in December, you can avoid a lot of the overhyped commercialism and replace it with a focus on Jesus, the solstice, nature, or nothing.

Enjoy it. You can be Christian and still enjoy all the secular Christmas stuff. You can be Jewish or Hindu or atheist or Pagan or anything else and still enjoy all the lights and the sparkle and the movies and the peppermint mochas. It doesn't mean you're any less of who you are and what you believe. It just means you're participating in something you experience as fun. (Even if it makes you feel a little cheesy, like buying a box of chocolates on Valentine's Day does.)

Pick and choose. It's totally ok to hate a lot of it and just ignore it while still watching every movie in the "12 Days of 007" series on tv. Or drive a different way so you don't have to see the Christmas tree in your town's main square but still drink eggnog and eat Christmas cookies. You have my permission to be inconsistent if you want to be. Who will care? It's not like there are any official Commercial Christmas Police.

Dealing with cultural promotion of Christmas in public schools is another issue entirely. In theory, in the United States, there isn't supposed to be promotion of any one religion or religious holiday in public schools, but many do Christmas programs, projects, trips, writing assignments about Santa Claus, etc. This can be painful for people who celebrate religious Christmas but not cultural Christmas, for those of other faiths, and for everyone else. And those who enjoy it are sometimes pained that others are not enjoying it because then they can't enjoy it fully. It becomes a big mess.

If you live in a country where Christmas isn't celebrated in public schools OR everyone's ok with Christmas being celebrated in public schools, breathe a sigh of relief.

The obvious solution would be to stop celebrating Christmas in public schools in the U.S. entirely, but that won't happen, so you'll probably be less conflicted if you decide what to do about it before the season starts. Here are four options:

Ignore it. Know that your kids are getting what you teach them at home, whether that's the nativity story or another story or a debunking of myths. Let what happens at school happen, and don't think about it too much. Obviously this is easier once your kids are older and don't believe everything they're taught in school.

Push back. Let your kids' school know that you want the freedom to teach your kids what you want them to know about Christmas, and that your children won't be participating in school Christmas activities. Talk to other parents and see if you can get them to push back on the school with you. (Don't forget that Christians who celebrate Jesus and aren't into Santa are on the same side of this as atheists and people of other faiths who don't want Christmas stuff in school, so you may have a bigger group than you think.)

Quietly subvert it. What if your kids just weren't there for the performances and projects? You could schedule trips, dentists' appointments, or other things that have to happen when your kids would be doing the activities at school. This only works for prescheduled activities, so your kids may still come home with letters written to Santa from language arts class, but you're minimizing the exposure without using excess energy.

Celebrate it. Just go whole hog into it. Tell your kids it's the Big American Christmas, and enjoy it for what it is, like anthropologists.

However you deal with the cultural promotion of Christmas, I hope that a brand new car with a big red bow on it appears mysteriously in your driveway on Christmas morning, paid for by someone else.

You are just so tired

I get it. Life is exhausting. And you're busy holding it together for everyone else.

Here's some wisdom from EPMD from the song "You Gots To Chill":

"If you're tired, then go take a nap."

No, really. Take a break. Sit down and put your feet up. Or get into your bed and take an actual nap. The house (or your office) will not burn down around you.

Self-care is IMPORTANT. If you burn out, what happens? Wouldn't it be better (for everyone) if you took some breaks, did some things that you like, and kept yourself feeling healthy and strong?

Go take a nap.

4 IMPORTANT CONCEPTS

There are a few other concepts that are important to keep in mind during the Christmas season, for your own mental state and for getting along with your family.

Managing your energy

Some people gain energy by being in contact with other people and lose energy by spending too much time alone. Some people lose energy by being around other people and gain energy by being alone.

Understanding AND HONORING which one of those you are can vastly improve your Christmas season, and understanding which of those your children and partner (if you have them) are can help everything.

People who gain energy by being with others need to make sure that they're getting enough real contact every day to stay feeling good. (The energy part really is about physical health. If you've ever had that "jumping out of your skin" from too much or too little human contact, you get it.) Just being in crowds of people or at busy parties won't do it--they need actual interaction. In fact, it can be more difficult for people who gain energy from interaction to be in huge crowds or concert situations, because they can't tune out the other people easily, but they also aren't getting real interaction.

So those who gain energy from interaction need to plan for enough small-group or one on one situations to fill their needs. Attending performances can be tiresome and overwhelming, and make them need more contact later to feel like their needs are being met.

People who lose energy by being with others need to make sure that they're planning in enough alone time to stay healthy. It's often safer to accept invitations for larger events that won't require much one-on-one interaction, such as concerts or large parties, because they can surf the crowd (so to speak) and not have to actually interact. They do not do as well in medium sized group situations in which they're expected to engage in intense interaction with several people.

Understanding these differences means that you can pick and choose which activities you do and which ones you sign your kids up for so everyone gets their needs met. It also means you won't have hurt feelings when someone doesn't want to do something you want to do, or asks you to do something you don't want to do.

Cheat sheet:

Those who gain energy from being with people should attend cocktail parties, dinners, office parties, one-on-one dates.

Those who gain energy from being alone should attend concerts and large parties, and one-on-one dates (with people who understand that they can't interact forever).

Since people are forced to attend office parties, the two types should buddy up so that the person who gains from interaction can protect the one who gains from alone time from too much interaction with bosses and co-workers. In exchange the one who gains from alone time should monitor the alcohol consumption of the one who gains from interaction to prevent embarrassment and career destruction.

If people of opposite types live together, the one who needs interaction should go out with friends while the other stays home alone, and neither should feel like there's anything wrong with that, since both sets of needs are being met.

If people of opposite types are planning an event together, make sure there's enough opportunity for interaction for one person and enough opportunity for the other one to hide in the garage getting people drinks.

Love languages

Have you ever done or given something to another person that really showed your love, but the other person wasn't that impressed? Or been given something or had the other person try to show you love in a way they obviously thought was great, but just didn't mean that much to you? It can be confusing and hurtful, and make you feel like you're not connecting with the other person.

The reason for that is that different people value different things and use different actions as ways of expressing love. If you and the person you are trying to express love to value the same things, everyone feels great about the exchange. If the two of you don't value the same things, there can be hurt feelings.

One easy-to-understand way of categorizing what different people value is Gary D. Chapman's idea of Love Languages. You can buy the original book or just search "love languages" on the internet to see what they are and to figure out which one you are and which ones your family members are. Once you figure this out, it will become so much easier to make everyone feel loved, and to accept what other people do in the spirit in which it's intended.

For example, if someone suggests stopping giving each other individual presents and instead doing an activity together, the people who value spending time together will think this is a great idea, the people who value gifts will feel hurt, and the people who value something else won't have an opinion.

Someone who values gifts will appreciate gifts and not like gift cards as much, while someone who doesn't value gifts may prefer gift cards to gifts.

Making decisions about who does what with whom and what you should spend your energy on, and how you should interpret loved ones' actions, all becomes much more clear when you understand what resonates with people.

Family roles

Chances are, if you're in a family of any sort, you've been playing out a role for years. This may be a role that dates back to your childhood. But that role probably has you pigeonholed as the smart one or the athletic one or the bad one, the late one, the one who always takes care of mom when she's drunk, the one everyone tells their problems to, the one no one expects much of, the one who has it all together.

Playing out these roles is preventing you and your siblings and the rest of your family from being as close to and honest with each other as you could be. If you stay in your own role, you never have to really interact and you never have to expose your true self.

This might not be the year for you to break out of your role. If you feel pressed or stressed this year, just sit back quietly and observe how the roles work in your family.

If you feel like you're ready to break out, though, try it. See what happens when you do something that doesn't conform to what everyone thinks your role would do. Give others the space and the invitation to do things that don't fit with their roles. Know that it might be uncomfortable to reach out of your role, and it might feel really awkward at first. The more you do it, the easier it gets. And if your family members can follow your lead and break out, you can really get to know each other and connect better.

5 NOT-SO-SHINY-THINGS

There are a few things that can make this season almost unbearable that deserve a special chapter, apart from the other stuff that's just challenging.

Truly difficult family

A lot of people have run-of-the-mill issues with family and family gatherings at Christmas that make them not look forward to being together. But some people have individual family members or family systems and patterns that are so difficult that they truly dread being in the middle of them during the holidays.

If you:

- can never win,
- feel bruised by interactions with a family member, and/or
- get a panicked feeling in your chest that you just can't explain and justify yourself properly,

you are dealing with a situation that's not just "oh, my family ha ha ha" like other people talk about.

If someone (or more than one person) in your family needs to create crises to be the hero, or needs to be the martyr, or creates situations in which you are required to jump through a bunch of hoops (and then you can't do it correctly), this is a sick system. It's a feedback loop that rewards laying traps for people and controlling you by making you never good enough and keeping you trying to earn approval or love.

You cannot win. And the harder you try, the more traumatic it is for you and the more they want from you.

The people in your family who do this most likely have no idea that they're doing it or that it's an unhealthy way of interacting with others. It's probably the way they were raised, so they think it's normal. They probably think they're helping you, and are convinced that without their guidance you'd fall apart.

You may even be convinced that they're right and that you're just a screw-up and that they know how to get you to stop messing things up, if you could only do what they want you to.

But this isn't true. You're not a screw-up. (If you were you would never have picked up this book to begin with because you wouldn't care about making things easier.) And the way to help someone improve is to be quietly supportive, not to make them feel anxious and pressured and like they're doing things incorrectly. (Yes, there are research studies in management, performance science, leadership, psychology, and medicine to prove this. Making someone feel bad in order to motivate them doesn't work.)

Putting you on the defensive for things you didn't do is called gaslighting.

You should not have to try to manage other people to get them to make you not feel bad. But if those people don't even realize that they're doing anything unhealthy or that they're gaslighting you, they can't stop. So you're the only one who can get out of this cycle.

Remember that the more you give and the more you explain, the more the person will ask from you and try to get you engaged and explaining. There is never an amount that you can try or give that will be enough to satisfy them, because they'll just keep moving the target and demanding more from you. So the way to minimize it is to hold your boundaries very very firm. Do not explain. Do what you want to do and then don't explain yourself. Don't justify. Hold your position and don't agree to keep working for the other person.

If it is too difficult or painful for you to hold a firm boundary and draw hard lines, the other alternative is not to show up. If you aren't there, then the other person can't push you. Yes, they can try by attempting to push you by phone or other means. And you may be afraid of what they're saying or thinking about you while you're not there. But your absence is a hard line that protects you. You can still be who you really are, without having to compromise and live to someone else's idea of who you are and who you should be.

It can be extremely difficult to recover from a lifetime of being told you're not good enough, even if you haven't been told that in words. Especially if you haven't been told that in words! Feeling--for years--like you just can't get it right and just can't measure up is painful, but you think it's your own fault. You don't always recognize it as abuse, especially because the person doing it to you may love you dearly and not have any idea that they're doing it. But that doesn't mean it isn't abusive to you. And that it doesn't affect your thought and behavior patterns. Growing up with the message that you don't measure up often leads you to find friends and romantic partners who don't think you measure up and who keep you working hard to earn their love. This means that you truly have no one who gives you a safe place to just be yourself--your family makes you work for it, and your friends and partner make you work to earn love, too.

This is not fair and it's not tenable, and it's no wonder you feel stressed and unhappy and like you're never doing enough. You can get out of this situation, though. First, spend some real, honest time thinking about how often this pattern plays out in your life, that someone makes it impossible for you to really win with them. Then, think about any relationships you have in which this is NOT the dynamic, and which feel healthy and nurturing to you. Start spending more energy and time in those relationships. Third, think about the relationships that do have this hurtful pattern and consider how you can limit the hurt and importance of these patterns in the context of the rest of the relationship with that person.

For Christmas this year it may be easier to go and play along like usual and then spend the next few months getting your head around it and making a plan. Or you may be ready to draw some hard lines either in person or by not showing up at all.

If this all sounds uncomfortably familiar, know that you aren't alone. This is a real thing. And you can break the cycle and feel good in your relationships again.

For more work on this, read *Codependent No More* by Melody Beattie.

Depression

I know I already mentioned depression, but, well, it takes over everything, doesn't it?

The thing about depression is that it skews your perception of things so that you can feel only a little out of sync with the rest of humanity or waaay out of sync, like you're an alien who sees things in such a fundamentally different way that it's impossible to connect with anyone else. (The irony of this, of course, is that so very many of us have depression that if we could only connect with each other the disease wouldn't be able to control us because we'd all have that connection. But we can't connect because the nature of depression is isolation. Like rain on your wedding day, truly.)

So you can go along all year with your normal depression and be hanging in there and finding meaning despite it all, but then the peppermint mochas come out and suddenly you're completely off-kilter and the inside of your head tastes burned and you can see into the terrifying core of the earth. In other words, the Christmas season seems to make everything way rougher for the average person with depression. And sometimes the exact stuff we do to try to not be sucked under makes it even worse.

The Xmas season is artificially heightened in so many ways, so it can exacerbate the feeling of being different from everyone else. If everything in December is bright and shiny and sparkling, and your norm with depression is a little muted, that muted can feel really inferior compared to all the sparkle. Even when you know that the sparkle is forced for most people and is a fabrication of capitalism that's going to be chopped off precisely at 11:59 pm on Christmas Day, your norm can feel extra bad relative to everything swirling around you.

Add to that just the simple physical slow-down: You may be stuck inside more because of colder or inclement weather, and there's less sunshine during the day so you're not able to do self-care including spending time outside and getting natural light therapy from the sun.

And then there's the cultural fetishization of family during the Christmas season, which feels out of sync for those of us who have to work through a regular schedule and maybe don't have a lot of family members around us all the time, or who have too many family members to coordinate, and still have to work hard to keep our own heads above water in terms of mood and mental health. It's an extra layer of struggle, this expectation that somehow simply having members of our families makes everything perfect and cozy. And that even if things are cozy we're not still depressed.

So you get worried that you're going into another bad phase with the depression. That your care routine is no longer working for no reason. That you've somehow done something wrong and now you're never going to not feel horrible again. If you already have anxiety along with your depression you get anxious about being depressed and anxious. If you usually "only" have depression you might become anxious about it, too.

Your sleep gets screwed up and your normal resilience goes way down and all the added stuff about the holiday season seems insurmountable--money, family dynamics, loneliness, expectations. And then you try to make yourself feel better by giving in to the sparkle swarming around you. You eat your emotions and they taste like eggnog and cookies and fudge. You drink more alcohol. You drink more coffee, especially peppermint mochas. Your body gets dehydrated and oversugared and starts to feel fatigued and even worse than usual.

So now you actually are more depressed than you were before, but the highs of the season make you even more unaligned, and it feels horrible and you feel horrible and it feels like there's no way out.

It's all a rebound effect. You start out at the same level you were in July, but then the general environment gets all cranked up so you feel like you're lower than usual, and then the coping mechanisms you use to try to feel normal again make you feel even worse.

Last year, Shannon Ford and I started writing an online Advent calendar for people who have depression, like us. We were basically writing what we wanted to hear, to make us feel like we weren't alone in the middle of it all. We heard from a lot of people who slipped us really quiet notes thanking us for putting it out there that it's possible to be depressed even during Christmas. It felt good enough that we're doing it again this year, and we're inviting you to read along with us at AdventCalendarForDepressedPeople.com.

There are some things you can do that might make you actually feel better during the Christmas season, at least enough to feel like you're maintaining and not drowning.

1. Stay meta. Understand that everything about this season is an utter fabrication, from the music piped through the sound systems everywhere you go to the flavors we're supposed to be eating to the emotions we're supposed to be feeling to the relationships we're supposed to be modeling our relationships after. Why, exactly, are we supposed to be happier to see family in December than at any other time of the year? Don't believe the hype. You're still you. Everyone else is still everyone else. December's just a month that ends in R.

2. Grinch it up. Or Scrooge it up, if you're not into green. It is totally 100% ok to not be in "the Christmas spirit." (Hey, if you were really into the Christmas spirit you'd be a teenager with a crisis pregnancy who was seeing visions of angels, forced to attend a big government registration process in a strange place resulting in giving birth to your potentially socially-ostracized baby in really uncomfortable conditions. Sounds fun!)

2a. It's ok to feel joy. When you're a person with depression, sometimes feeling joy almost feels like a betrayal, or like it must not really have been all that bad somehow. That's just not true--you can feel great sometimes and still have depressive periods, and you can have depressed periods sometimes and still feel joy a lot of the time. If joy comes to you, snatch it up and wave it around, in the Christmas season and whenever else it happens.

3. Find some kind of meaning. If there is something about this season that is inherently meaningful to you, put your time and energy into that. Let everything else go. Whether that is the birth of Jesus or simply coming around the corner of the year so the days start getting longer on December 22, or anything else that you find meaningful about this season, focus on that. If there is nothing you find meaningful about this season, then go back to step 2 and just opt out.

4. Focus on your health. There's a lot of focus on eating and drinking this month anyway, so why not direct that into eating and drinking things that are going to make your body feel better? Say no to all the sugar. (The rebound cycle will make you feel disgusting. You're already scraping your tongue on the roof of your mouth just reading this.) Make extra sure you're getting a lot of water in. Manage your caffeine smartly. Be strategic about alcohol. Get in six servings of vegetables a day. Come up with something that feels comforting but doesn't make your body feel bad, like cinnamon tea or clementines or pomegranates or roasted chestnuts, and go to that thing when you get the urge to take comfort in food.

5. Move. Doing 20 minutes a day of yoga or pilates or walking, every day of this month, will make you feel radically better and will offset every inadvertent hearing of "The Little Drummer Boy" you suffer through. Your body is good to you and it deserves to be moved in a purposeful way every day.

6. Talk about it. It's ok to have depression. Some of the best people do. You're allowed to talk about it, and talking about it makes it less scary and less painful and more something that you're living with instead of being victimized by. If you talk about it and anyone gives you the "try harder" or "but it's Christmas!" line, just move on to someone else. A LOT of us are in the same boat and totally get it. And we're happy (get it?) to talk or IM or text about it when you just need to complain about it.

7. Keep your eyes open for the rest of us. Instead of standing in line or sitting in traffic thinking about how different and alone you are, slow your breathing and look around so you notice the other depressed people around you. There are so many of us slogging through this month with you. Even if we can't connect, we're all connected. You, too.

HEY: If it feels really too heavy and you don't know if you can hold on, text the crisis hotline and they'll text you through it so you can hold on. Text the word "go" to 741741 or search "suicide hotline" on the internet for a number to text in your country.

General life dissatisfaction

You know what I mean. You're doing all the right things and you're walking through the days and maybe you even have fun on weekends. You love your family and everyone thinks you're a happy, successful person. But there's just something wrong. And you don't know what you could do that would make it all feel connected and meaningful somehow.

This is big. It's huge, and it's the rest of your life, and it's the difference between just living and really using your life. It's surviving vs. being satisfied.

How do you create meaning? I'm working on a longer process for this, but I think the first step is to identify that this is what you're feeling: a mismatch between what you spend your time doing and what feels meaningful to you. It is entirely possible to be doing things that are calibrated to create certain emotions, or to be serving people you love, or to be doing all the things that you're supposed to do to get to where you want to go, and still feel empty and like what you're doing isn't meaningful to you.

Anything that's out of alignment in your life tends to come to a head around the end of the year, and that's exacerbated by being around family who may see you in a way you don't see yourself. (This is why people tend to come out around the holidays or ask for divorces at this time of year--misalignment feels like deception and they need to get it out into the open.) It hurts more at this time of year to feel like you're wasting time or wasting your talents or spending yourself on things that aren't giving you what you thought they would.

Now that you know that you're dissatisfied and something needs to change, what are you going to do about it? If this were a novel or a movie, you'd have the big epiphany right exactly now about what you should be doing, and you'd sit down and make a list of steps and then you'd dive in. But this is real life, so instead, you're going to sit with this for the rest of the month. You're going to watch yourself carefully, like you would someone you were considering dating, and you're going to pay attention to what you do during the day.

You're going to watch yourself and think about the things you do because you're supposed to and the things you do because you enjoy them and the things you do because they're just part of who you are. Let yourself have opinions and emotions about your daily movements and tasks. Let yourself be disloyal to ideas you've had about yourself and your path for a long time. Spend time pursuing the question "What if?"

Don't shortcut this. It's really ok, good even, to feel uncomfortable about being in the middle of the wrong story (or even the wrong chapter of the right story). And you owe it to yourself to spend enough time figuring out why it's wrong that you can eventually figure out how to jump (or edge) into the right story. Since the Christmas season brings everything to a fever pitch anyway, make use of that intensity tell you where the biggest rubs are between what you're doing and what you should be doing.

And yes, I said "should." I don't mean should as in what your parent thought would be appropriate for you. I mean should as in what makes you you, and maximizes who you are. What makes you most valuable. Even if it scares you, and even if it doesn't scare you at all.

Don't run away from this feeling. Don't shop it away or eat it away or drink it away or stay so busy that you can't feel it. Let it tell you what's really the problem. You've come this far, so you don't have to fix everything right away. You can take some time to make sure it's right for you.

6 CHRISTMAS SEASON HOLIDAYS

These are holidays you may want to consider adding to your mix of activities and celebrations during this time of year.

Candletime

You may already be familiar with Candletime, a holiday I created in 2009 to give people the opportunity to be cozy and sparkly without having to start all the commercial Christmas pressure early. It's a buffer between Halloween and the US-based post-Thanksgiving Christmas season start.

Candletime is completely non-religious and can be celebrated by anyone who enjoys light.

Candletime runs from November 1 (the day after Halloween) through the night before US Thanksgiving, although if you're not in the US you can run it through whenever you want to. (You can start it whenever you want to, too, but I like to finish Halloween before starting Candletime.)

The rules of Candletime are simple. Every evening when you're home, light candles (or switch on electric candles) to feel cozy. Sit and enjoy your candles while drinking a beverage of your choice. Popular beverages for Candletime include tea (hot, sweet, or unsweet), hot cider, cold cider, water, wine, beer, hot cocoa, coffee, soda, and bourbon.

Candletime can be celebrated alone or with others, and you can observe as many days of the holiday period as you choose. You can blow out the candles whenever you want (they don't have to burn down on their own).

For more information about Candletime, Like the Candletime Facebook page at https://www.facebook.com/Candletime or check out the Candletime page on the web at http://askmoxie.org/candletime/

Advent

Some Christian denominations celebrate the holiday season called Advent, or "coming," as a season of waiting and preparation for the birth of Jesus. Advent consists of the four Sundays before Christmas Day and the days in between those Sundays. (Advent often starts the Sunday after US Thanksgiving.)

Whether or not you are a Christian, I invite you to incorporate some aspect of Advent, or waiting and preparation, into your Christmas season plans.

The point of Advent is to be quiet and get ourselves ready for the birth of Jesus. If you don't believe in Jesus, you can use Advent as a time of waiting quietly and becoming ready for the next new thing. (There's a reason Christmas was deliberately celebrated right near the Solstice and the New Year. It's a time of new beginnings.)

Traditional Advent celebrations include making an Advent wreath containing four candles (three purple and one pink, or four blue, in the modern version) and lighting the candles while singing "O Come, O Come Emmanuel" and then reading a Bible verse. Lutheran pastor Paige Evers has written an excellent and accessible series on the four weeks of Advent and simple celebrations appropriate for kids of all ages. It can be found at http://christmased.com/christmased/?tag=paige+evers

Another way to celebrate Advent is by doing daily readings. You can google for lists of readings, or use a book of readings. My favorite religious Advent books are *Advent and Christmas Wisdom from Henri J.M. Nouwen: Daily Scripture and Prayers together with Nouwen's Own Words* and *God is in the Manger: Reflections on Advent and Christmas* by Dietrich Bonhoeffer.

My favorite non-religious books for reading during Advent are all appropriate for both adults and kids (with explanation):

A Child's Christmas in Wales by Dylan Thomas
A Christmas Carol by Charles Dickens
Earth, My Likeness: Nature Poetry of Walt Whitman

Another classic way to celebrate Advent is with an Advent calendar. A traditional Advent calendar is a picture with small numbered cutout windows that you open in order, one each day, to reveal another part of the story of the nativity story. Modern Advent calendars, however, include everything from pieces of chocolate to Legos to whisky samples.

You and your family will enjoy opening Advent calendars, and may even enjoy making them. If you have children, be sure to have one Advent calendar per child until your kids are old enough to share joyfully, unless you want the calendars to cause less joy than disappointment.

Shannon Ford and I write an online Advent calendar of little readings for people who are depressed (or who want to understand and support people who are depressed). We do it at AdventCalendarForDepressedPeople.com and it runs from the beginning of Advent through January 6. You can read all of the entries from last year before we start this year.

Advent is a time of waiting and preparation, but NOT a self-improvement challenge, so it violates the spirit of quiet waiting and exploration to use it for self-improvement projects like going off sugar or training for a race or using positive self-talk. It is, however, appropriate to do daily practices like meditating, walking in nature, or other daily rituals that feed your soul and bring you peace.

St. Nicholas Day/Krampus

The feast day of St. Nicholas is celebrated on December 6 in
Germany and other European countries. Saint Nicholas was the
Bishop of Myra (in Greece) in the 4th century ACE. There were many
divine works attributed to him, but his big claim to fame was leaving
little surprise presents for people (see: Love Languages). Over the
centuries, Saint Nicholas--a bishop who left people trinkets to
encourage them--turned into Santa Claus--a mythical creature who
flew around the world in one night leaving presents for kids who
were well-behaved. (Talk about missing the main point of the story.)

People who celebrate Saint Nicholas Day do it on December 6 with
small presents, sometimes left in the recipient's shoe. (Eastern
Orthodox Christians celebrate on December 19.)

The same kind of storytelling and lore that evolved St. Nicholas into
Santa Claus also celebrated the dark side of the giving story by
creating a devilish foil to St. Nicholas: the Krampus. The Krampus is
allegedly a bright red half human-half goat figure who roamed the
European countryside looking for misbehaving children. Children
who behaved would wake up in their beds on the morning of
December 6 with a present in their shoe from St. Nick. Children who
misbehaved would be stuffed into a sack and taken by the Krampus
off to his lair on the night of December 5 and never heard from
again.

You can celebrate St. Nicholas Day with people of all ages: Have
them leave their shoes outside their bedroom doors or right in front
of your front door when they go to bed on December 5, and when
they wake up on December 6 there should be a small present (toy car
or figurine or bar of fancy chocolate or something similarly
not-expensive) in one shoe.

You can celebrate Krampus with older kids and teens and adults by
joking around about being taken, eating spicy things, dressing up as
Krampus, and generally just being a smartass on the evening of

December 5. (Make sure everyone gets their St. Nicholas presents i: their shoes the next morning anyway.)

Solstice/Yul

The December Solstice is the shortest day of the year, and has been celebrated as the day the darkness begins to recede and we move toward longer days again. Yul/Yule is the name of the European celebrations of the December solstice. Once Christmas was officiall designated to be at the time of the solstice, Yule became the name o the Christmas season in European countries.

Traditional celebrations of Yul included a lot of drinking, burning the Yule log, roasting pigs, and other celebratory activities from medieval Europe. Modern pagans tend to focus on the more natura aspects of the time period and incorporate a lot of lights and give gifts to celebrate the solstice.

Twelve Days of Christmas

Traditionally, the twelve days between Christmas Day and Epiphan (the day the three kings are supposed to have visited toddler Jesus, celebrated on January 6th) are celebrated as the Christmas season b the church.

Different Christian sects have had different celebrations of this time period, but one common way of celebrating is to give small gifts, on on each day of the twelve days, each signifying a month in the new year.

Other ways to celebrate include reading or watching a performance of Shakespeare's *Twelfth Night,* or doing any other twelve-related practice over the 12 days following Christmas. Film festivals, baking, volunteering, or doing any other activities you can do for 12 days in a row would add meaning to that time period.

Some people find that if they shift their Christmas celebration from a big hoopla leading up to Christmas to starting their celebration on Christmas Eve or Christmas Day and then extending through the twelve days, everything is more relaxed and fun and less frenetic and stressful. (I did that accidentally one year just by not putting up a Christmas tree or any decorations at home, so then when I got it together on Christmas Eve it was suddenly like, "Whoa, Christmas!") Even if you don't have time off work after Christmas Day, you could still do stuff like visiting Christmas exhibits and activities in the days after Christmas, and it'll be more relaxed then than if you go earlier in the month. And without the anticipation of a big present frenzy, you can enjoy more even tempers and less tightly-wound emotions.

7 IF YOU HAVE CHILDREN: CREATING A CHRISTMAS FOR YOUR KIDS THAT IS AS GREAT AS THE ONES YOU HAD GROWING UP, OR BETTER

For a lot of us, there's a lingering sense of guilt that the Christmases we're giving our kids aren't as great as the ones we had as kids, ourselves. Or that we could be creating Christmases for our kids that are fantastic (even if our own childhood Christmases weren't great) but are somehow missing the mark. That may be reality or it may just be our perceptions, but it's causing us anxiety, pain, or other bad feelings, so we owe it to ourselves to get to the bottom of it.

As with everything else in life, they key to knowing how to act is figuring out where the boundaries are. So let's walk through this step by step and find a way to make a Christmas season we feel is worthy of our kids.

Questions to answer:

1. Are the Christmases you're creating for your kids actually not as good as the ones you had as a child, or is this just your perception?

a. Your kids have never experienced the Christmases you had as a child. Are they happy with the Christmases they have now? (If so, then a comparison doesn't matter.)

b. Is it possible that you have a sparkly filter on when you remember your childhood Christmases but an HDTV hyper-realistic filter on for Christmases now, that will always make the past seem better, no matter what the reality is?

2. What is preventing you from creating Christmases for your kids that are as good as you want them to be?

3. What if you were ok with not creating Christmases that were as great as you think they should be? Could you be ok with that? Or would that require letting go of something you're not willing to let go of?

4. Are the things that are preventing you from creating a great Christmas for your kids actually preventing it, or are you just looking at things from one angle? For example, if you said that lack of money was preventing you from creating the Christmas you want to give your kids, is there a way to create that same feeling for them without needing to use so much money? Or if you said that that not being together with your children's other parent was preventing you from creating a great Christmas for them, is there a way you could create a Christmas that felt great to them without being together?

Let's dig into that a little more deeply here.

Think about either your amazing Christmases from your childhood or the ideal Christmas you'd like to give your child. Write down how your child would **feel** when experiencing the different parts of that Christmas.

Now, think about what it was in your ideal Christmas vision that caused those feeling in the child.

Pause for a moment before we go into the step about recreating those feelings. Think about your children's personalities AND the things they need and value most. You know what those are, and they may be different for each of your children if you have more than one.

What feelings would be most special and important for your child to have during the ideal Christmas?

Do those intersect with the feelings you identified in your own ideal Christmas for them?

Is it possible that the Christmases you create for your kids are already hitting the emotions that are most important to them, but you just didn't realize that because you were thinking about the feelings that are important to you? If that's the case, stop for a minute to think about that, pat yourself on the back for instinctively doing exactly what your kids needed, remind yourself to trust your own intuition more often because it's good, and then skip the rest of this section and move on.

If not, then refine, right here, the feelings you want to create for the ideal Christmas for your kids. They should include the feelings that are important for your kids, but can also include the feelings you listed earlier:

NOW. Think about the things that you wrote that were preventing you from creating the ideal Christmas. What resources (physical, financial, personal, emotional, friends and family) do you have that either make up for those blocks or are better than those blocks? (Examples: ideal family is loud and boisterous, but your real family is small and very connected. Ideal family has two parents together, but real family has a happy parent who is able to be free with the kids and really focus on them.)

Those things that you just wrote down as strengths are your toolkit. So let's use your tools to build the feelings that you want to create in your kids. In one of the upcoming sections of this workbook we're going to pick a theme for your Christmas season, and then we're going to pick activities in a bunch of categories. Think of this as a parallel process, so keep the feelings you want to create in mind when you pick the themes, and use these feelings to help you choose activities.

YOU DON'T HAVE TO DO ALL OF THIS NOW. You might come up

with some things right now, but don't push too hard. Maybe do the rest of the workbook and see if that jogs anything for you, and then come back when you've got it. Remember that you're having a looooong conversation with your kids as they grow up, so you don't have to hit it perfectly (in your opinion) this year. Your feeling of moving closer to ideal is the important thing.

To create this feeling: we are going to do:

To create this feeling: we are going to do:

To create this feeling: we are going to do:

To create this feeling: we are going to do:

8 CREATING YOUR PLAN

So far we've been doing a lot of prep working dealing with expectations, underlying issues, our feelings of inadequacy or resentment, and exploring some other options to focus on during the season.

In this chapter we put it all together and start making decisions about how we want the season to go.

What You Want The Christmas Season To Feel Like

Now that we've explored how you currently feel about Christmas, some of the issues you may have with Christmas, and creating a Christmas that feels like you want it to feel for your kids, let's draw out how you'd like Christmas to feel to you.

When I hear the word "Christmas," I'd like to feel:

During the Christmas season and on Christmas Day I'd like to feel:

I'd like my energy level during the Christmas season to be:

I'd like to take the following away from the Christmas season:

Making Your Plan

We've explored the feelings you have and want to have, and dealt with some special issues for you during the whole long Christmas season, so let's dig into the meat of this, which is creating a plan that makes the entire season work for you and your family.

There are two parts to this. The first is choosing what you want the season to be about for you, and the second is choosing the activities you'll engage in during the whole long season.

I am going to urge you to choose the things you really feel attracted to and get excited about. The exact reason the holiday season is so difficult for everyone is because of feelings of obligation and a mismatch with your values, so DO NOT do that to yourself. Go with your gut here and choose both the themes and activities you feel good about.

(If going with your own desires and preferences doesn't work out, you can always stuff yourself back into a box of obligation next year.)

BEFORE WE MAKE THIS PLAN:

Write down any and all anxiety you may have about doing something different this year, and taking any potential heat from family or friends about not doing the same thing you've done for years:

Now, write down your secret joy (or maybe your secret "neener neener neener") about stepping off the hamster wheel and finding your own meaning:

Choose The Theme of Your Holiday Season

I've been saying "Christmas Season" this entire time and now I'm saying "Holiday Season." What gives? Well, here's where you get to decide what this is all about for you. And it may be Christmas, specifically, but it may just be that it's a holiday season, or it may be something else entirely. So for this one section of the workbook I'll leave the language open.

If this season is going to have any meaning aside from rampant consumer excess, you have to give it meaning for you. And that means making a deliberate choice about what that meaning is going to be. Choose at least one but no more than three themes for the season, stick to those themes, and the season will come together for you as a celebration of something you enjoy and find meaning in.

Here are some suggested themes, but of course you can come up with your own.

Jesus: Well, it's Christmas, right? If you're a Christian, the birth of Jesus is a big deal and the whole point of the holiday. If you choose Jesus, really choose Jesus, and do the entire story through the birth (at age-appropriate levels for everyone in your family). You might also explore the other Christian traditions of Advent and the Twelve Days of Christmas (the twelve days are AFTER Christmas, not before).

You might consider buying or making a nativity scene and putting it in your house, visiting a "living nativity scene" put on by a local church, participating in or attending a nativity pageant at a church, reading books about the whole story (from the visit from the angel to Mary to tell her she was going to have a child through the visit from the academics from the Far East to see Jesus), listening to music about the birth, making a birthday cake for Jesus for Christmas morning, and exploring the story in other ways.

Giving: There is a lot to explore about giving during the holiday season, everything from the Santa story and mythology based in the life of St. Nicholas to the big onslaught of presents (which is fantastic if that's what you like) to more quieter ways of giving, both to individuals and to support groups and charities.

You could create, for you and your family, an entire season of focus on different ways of giving to other people, including books about giving, planning what you will give to others (individual presents and to the community and to charities), ideas about value and gifts that cost money compared to gifts that don't cost money, and a deliberate focus on giving without an expectation of receiving.

Light: Light is a great theme alone or to add on to other themes. It goes perfectly with Jesus (who is the Light of the World) or Nature or Magic or Festivity. It's also a big part of Hanukkah and Candletime and Diwali, if you're celebrating those during the holiday season. Create and find light during the winter with candles, lights (you can put up strings of lights whether or not you have a Christmas tree), and mirrors to reflect light. Drive around looking at the lights people put up on their houses, put up lights outside, go look at light displays at your local zoo, and observe the stars. Pay attention to sunrises and sunsets, and look for sparkle everywhere.

Nature: Nature is quiet and beautiful and still-alert at this time of year. How is your local natural area different during December than it is during the rest of the year? Does it feel like it's waiting? How can you connect to it? Going out for hikes and nature walks, bringing nature into your house (a Christmas tree, boughs, a wreath, leaves, pinecones, logs, flowers, stones, or anything else that's part of your natural habitat) is one way of celebrating nature. Another way would be to increase your focus on being environmentally responsible and reusing and consuming less (which goes along nicely with the Giving theme). Since the Solstice (December 22 this year) is a celebration of nature, you may want to incorporate Solstice celebration elements. A great resource for studying nature with kids is *Nature Study for the Whole Family* by Laurel Dodge.

Connection: You can connect with family, friends, your community, or the world, but the connection theme emphasizes human relationships and spending time with those we love. You can celebrate the connection theme by inviting people to spend time with you, individually, in small groups, or in parties, throughout the Christmas season. You can also increase connection by sending cards and letters and communicating electronically and by phone. The connection theme makes everything seem warmer, busier, more complicated, but happier.

Quiet: The Christmas season can be the loudest month or the quietest month, depending on the activities you choose to do and the things you surround yourself with. A perfect companion to the Light, Nature, or Jesus themes, spending a month being quiet and celebrating quiet with your family could be just the renewal you need.

What is your definition of quiet? Is it silence? Or stillness? Or gentle sounds? Maybe you want to spend the Christmas season exploring what quiet means to you, and how much of that actually has to do with sound and how much has to do with other forms of energy.

Mystery: Christmas is filled with mystery. Whether it's the incarnation of God as Jesus, how Santa can visit every child in the world in 24 hours, or how still and beautiful the world is during a nighttime snowfall, there is so much that happens under the surface and doesn't always reveal itself. Celebrate the mystery of the season by wondering, by appreciating the unusual, and by noticing things you don't usually notice.

Joy: Celebrating joy in the middle of a busy Christmas season is primarily about giving fewer things space in your brain and life than about adding things. Think carefully about what gives you joy--and what gives your family joy--and put limits on what else you allow during the Christmas season. Make a specific plan with your family about what you engage in and consume, and choose only the things that actually make you happy. Watch your ratio of joy to pain increase!

Magic: The holiday season can be magical for a lot of reasons, and if that's something you want to capture you can turn it into a theme for the whole season. There are all kinds of magic-related stories for the season, from the nativity story to the Santa story, to Polar Express, to all the variants of A Christmas Carol. You can create magic for and with your family in your own house, and bring magic to other people with hidden good deeds.

Luxury: Luxury is abundance and warmth combined. The key to luxury is simplicity, so if you can't achieve that this year because of prior commitments, plan ahead to disentangle yourself so you can choose luxury for next year.

Festivity: Wish the entire Christmas season could be one long party? It can, if you want it to! Plan ahead, pace yourself, and don't overspend, and you can, truly, keep the party going. Remember to keep everyone on a regular sleep schedule, drink a lot of water, and limit sugar so everyone's immune systems keep running well. Then celebrate!

Your own theme: Is there something you want to choose as a theme that I didn't list? Go for it. (And when the season's over email me and let me know how it went and if I should include your theme on the list in the workbook next year.)

For the holiday season I am choosing the theme(s):

(Hey, seriously, no more than three. Unless you have no full-time job and no children or pets, are in perfect health, have unlimited funds and a whole gang of people who will celebrate with you but who take care of their own laundry and food. Otherwise, more than three themes is going to get too confusing and stressful, and the whole point is for this to be fun and not stressful.)

Choose The Activities For Your Christmas Season

Now it's time to choose the activities you'll do for the season. I've chosen five activity categories, but you do NOT have to do all of them. In fact, I recommend cutting out one of these categories for every child under 3, chronic illness, or job in crisis mode that you have. If I had to choose only two categories to engage in, I'd choose a Daily Practice and The Day. I know some of you doing this workbook are going to add in all kinds of other categories and I can't stop you, so just don't stress yourself out.

The categories:

- A Daily Practice
- A Service Project
- A Connection
- The Day
- Wild Card

You'll notice that all of these categories have different levels of commitment, different rhythms, and can take place separately from each other.

A Daily Practice

This stems from the celebration of Advent, but you can choose almost anything you want as a daily practice. One of the traditional Advent observances of candlelighting and/or reading, continuing Candletime in the evenings through the Christmas season, reading a story or poem every day, writing a story or poem every day, singing a song, writing a letter to someone, listening to music, meditating, sitting quietly while drinking a cup of tea for 20 minutes, doing some form of movement.

As long as the purpose is to do something every day, not to work on a self-improvement project (like training for a race), the contemplative waiting will bring you some moments of relaxation and peace.

What daily practice (either without or including your family) will you participate in this Christmas season?

A Service Project

Big or small, one-time or ongoing, a service project will make your Christmas season better. There are all kinds of service you can engage in, everything from serving at a homeless shelter on Thanksgiving and Christmas Day to picking a family from the Angel Tree at the mall to sponsoring a single mom and her family through a church to asking friends to bring food to donate to a food bank to collecting money to send to Heifer Fund to helping at an animal shelter to doing maintenance work at a nature preserve. Use the number of people in your family and ages of any kids to help you determine how involved you can be and how much time and money you can spend, then pick a project, talk about it, and do it.

What service project will you take on this Christmas season?

A Connection

Some people are lucky enough to be connected deeply with family and friends they love, but the rest of us have to be intentional about creating and nurturing relationships with people we want to be close to. The Christmas season gives us a wonderful chance to go deeper with people we want to be closer to by specifically and consistently reaching out to them and inviting them to spend time with us, both casually and in a more structured setting.

Choose someone you want to deepen your connection to, and make a consistent effort to reach out to that person during the Christmas season. If you have children and they're old enough, they may want to choose people to reach out to during the Christmas season as well.

Who will you choose to deepen your connection with this Christmas season?

The Day

First of all, your Christmas Day does not actually have to be December 25. Maybe you're working (and an enormous thank you to all who work on Christmas Day), or family can't all gather on that day, or your children are with their other parent, so you're having your official Christmas on another day. That's great. YOUR official Christmas is the day we're talking about as The Day.

Plan the day you want to have. If this means getting up and putting on nice clothes and going to church and then going to a relative's house for a big meal, do that. If this means staying in your pajamas, ordering in Chinese food and watching A Christmas Story six times in a row, do that. If this means making a special breakfast, then exchanging one or two small gifts and then going for a hike in the woods, do that.

How do you want Christmas Day to feel for you and your family? That's the day you should have.

Plan a day that honors the themes you've chosen, and includes elements that the people you're planning for will enjoy. And please consider dropping activities that no one is connected to or enjoys. This isn't the only day of the year that you can do almost anything you've traditionally done on Christmas Day (unless it's some external event that only happens that one day every year), but doing it other days might be more fun or meaningful because it isn't being done out of obligation.

What would be your fantasy Christmas Day?

What can you do on Christmas Day, realistically? (Try to get as close to your fantasy as economically and logistically possible.)

Wild Card

There's something that's important to you that I haven't talked about. Maybe it's performing or listening to live music, or going to see The Nutcracker or The Harlem Nutcracker, or visiting a certain market, or taking your children to have their picture taken with Santa, or making 15 dozen tamales to give to family and friends, or throwing a party on Boxing Day, participating in Dia de los Tres Reyes at your church, or making your great-grandmother's black walnut cake. Whatever it is, choose something that you genuinely like doing, that makes the Christmas season feel special to you.

What is your special wild card activity this Christmas season?

Now, take these activities you've chosen, and figure out what planning you need to do to make them happen. For example, what foods will you need to buy and people will you need to invite if one o your activities is throwing a party? What preparation will you need to do for your service project? Will you need to buy a book or Advent calendar (or make an Advent calendar) to do your daily practice? List out what you'll need to prep next to each activity.

Other Categories

Aside from the five activity categories, there are some other things you'll need to consider while you're planning your Christmas season. Being specific about deciding how to work them will cause you less stress and more fun. So don't skip this section.

Gifts

You probably, unless you live completely alone or with some very special people, need to give at least some gifts to some people this Christmas season.

While it is important to choose things people will like, it is more important to give gifts that you can afford to give. None of your recipients would be happy receiving a gift from you if they knew that it was hurting you financially to give it to them. (And if you are giving gifts to people who would be happy at your being hurt financially, stop giving them gifts. And cut off contact with them, if you can.)

Please only give gifts that you can afford.

This leads us to the question: What is your budget?

Realistically, what is the dollar (or your country's currency) amount you can spend on gifts this year and not feel bad on December 26 (or January 1 or 15 or 31)?

If it is $5, write down $5. If it is $5,000, write down $5,000.

(It's probably in between those numbers.)

Write it down here:

Now circle it.

Now, write down a list of all the people you feel like you should give gifts to:

Now, go back through that list and circle the people who will know and care, or to whom you feel obliged, to spend a certain amount of money on a gift for. (And don't assume that's everyone. I would be thrilled if someone gave me a Spotify playlist they'd spent the time choosing for me, which costs nothing. Throw in a fair trade chocolate bar and I'd be even more excited. Total cost of under $5 to make me feel loved and happy. I know there are a lot of people like me out there, so you definitely have some on your list of gift recipients.) Write down next to each of those circled people how much you need to spend on each.

Add up those numbers. If your sum is smaller than the number you wrote down for your budget, you're golden! If your sum is larger than the number you wrote down for your budget, you're going to have to make some choices. Go back through the list of circled people and start cutting. Choose some priorities for who you lower the amounts you spend on, and go through and make cuts.

Add up your numbers again. Are you below your budgeted amount? Are you below your budget amount by enough that you will have a little something left to buy chocolate bars for your non-circled people? If not, go make another round of cuts.

Now, go fill in for all the non-circled people what you'd like to give them and what those things will cost. (Don't forget to be realistic about time if you're planning to make any gifts. You really don't want to be knitting the second sleeve at midnight on Christmas Eve. Not that that's happened to me.)

If your total for the circled people and the un-circled people is smaller than your budget number, you are in luck! Start down your list now buying/making gifts, wrap as you buy, and you'll coast into an easy gift-giving finale.

If your total is above your budget number, it's time for more cuts. If this is really hard for you, you might be feeling out of balance in your relationships, because the money is feeling more important to you than the relationships, and you might want to dig into why. Your family and friends love you, no matter how much money you have, what you spend on gifts, even whether you give them a gift or not. Al they want is you.

Decorations

It's easy to say, "oh, decorations," and decide you're either a person who goes big with crazy sparkle and décor or a person who really does nothing. (And it's easy to feel like you need to justify your position by making it a philosophical choice.) But there's nothing trivial about being intentional about how you want your living space to feel to you. Living in a place that feels good, and makes you feel comfortable and happy, and makes your family feel comfortable and happy, is good for you. And conveying that there's something interesting or unusual or special about the Christmas season by changes in your living environment is a way to signify change to yourself and your family.

Go back to the themes you picked, and use those to help you decide if you want to make your living space look, smell, sound, and feel an special way. The Light theme lends itself to decorations, obviously, but you can bring elements of nature into your house for the look and smells of that theme (and a Christmas tree is both nature and lights). If your theme is Jesus, you probably want to incorporate images from the nativity story into your living space. There are all kinds of ways to add magic and mystery and luxury and any other theme to your living space, too, that don't take much time or money if you stay focused on what you really like.

You probably have an image in your mind of how you want things to be in your living space. Write it down, and even if it's not completely achievable given time and other constraints, you can get closer to it than you would if you didn't articulate it.

How do you want your living space to look?

How do you want your living space to feel?

How do you want your living space to smell?

How do you want your living space to taste?

How do you want your living space to sound?

Daily Rhythm

Do you like it to be busy and filled with people at Christmas? Or do you like things to be more quiet and restful? Do you like having more activities than usual? Or more time to spend relaxing or reading and thinking?

Often our schedules become much more crowded during the Christmas season, which filters down and makes our minutes and hours more stress-filled and packed. Picking and choosing which activities we do will help with that, but it will also help if we can determine if we like the feeling of festive busyness, or prefer calm. Sometimes people who prefer busyness allow the obligations to pile up, thinking that will create the busyness they like, when what they actually want is the busyness of happy people around, not a bunch of obligations to slog through. So they find themselves stressed and unhappy without understanding why. (People who prefer calm and quiet usually know exactly why all the obligations stress them out.)

If you're a person who likes the feeling of "bustle," be careful that you aren't adding obligation but thinking it's pleasant busyness.

How would the rhythm of your day go, during the Christmas season?

Does that mean you need more to do than you're doing now, the same amount, or less to do?

What can you clear off your schedule by just saying no? ("I can't work it into the family schedule" is the perfect, non-arguable excuse.)

If you want a peppier, busier Christmas, do you need more people around you than you usually have? If so, how can you be around happy people? (Inviting them to your house, going to parties or gatherings in other locations, etc.)

If you want a more calm, relaxed Christmas, what can you do to protect your emotional, physical, and mental space?

What do you need to clear off your schedule RIGHT NOW so that you aren't feeling pressured and jammed in the middle of December?

Your Secret Wish

There is something that you really want to do or have or have happen to you. Write it down here. If you need to tell someone, email or tweet it to me.

Your Master List

My Christmas season is going to be:

The feelings I want to create in my kids are:

The theme(s) for my Christmas season:

My activities:

Daily Practice:

Service Project:

Connection:

The Day:

Wild Card:

Special Kid Activities:

___ Check when you have your gift list planned.

___ Check when your gifts are completed.

Decoration theme:

Daily Rhythm:

Creating a Calendar For Yourself

There are calendars and lists and schedules of when you should do what to be "ready" for Christmas all over the place, but those all assume that you're doing the same kind of Christmas the creator of the calendar is. Which is almost certainly not true. Let's give you the most peaceful, fulfilling Christmas season possible for you by creating a calendar just for you and what you've decided to do.

Choose your calendar. Are you a Gmail calendar person? Wall calendar? Bullet journal? Planner? Some other online system? Choose your weapon. (If you don't usually use a calendar, consider making a list of dates chronologically and then posting it somewhere.)

First add in one-time events that have to happen on a certain date. Performances, trips, school events, parties, any other events with a set date. (Optional: Make events that you just have to show up for with no prior prep one color on your calendar, and make events that require prep another color.)

If there are things you have to do to prep for any of these events, add the prep in to the calendar. Give things like food shopping or cleaning a specific date and time so that you spend the time to do them.

Then add in longer-term projects. If you're doing a Daily Practice that lends itself to being scheduled in, add that. Long cooking or crafting projects. Decorating or major cleaning.

Now, add in some rest periods for yourself. Think about what relaxes and recharges you, whether that's alone time, alone time with family or being with other people. Schedule it in now so you don't get crunched.

Last, add in events that don't require specific date. Choose a date and schedule them in around everything else you've already added. (Optional: Use the same color system to distinguish events that you just show up for from events that require prep.) Schedule in any prep you need to do for these events.

Now you have a calendar of only things you care about. If you're offered anything else to do you know exactly whether you have the time to do it or not. (Don't hesitate to say you're too busy if it doesn't sound like enough fun to make it worthwhile.)

GET CHRISTMASED

9 BUT WAIT!

There's less.

After I pulled you through all those decisions about creating a carefully-concocted holiday season, what if I told you you don't have to do any of it? Or that you could do ONE THING and that might make you just as peaceful and satisfied as working a theme and doing multiple activities?

If you were going to do only one thing, throughout the entire Xmas season, what would it be?

(Think about it.)

THANK YOU FOR WORKING THROUGH THE GET CHRISTMASED WORKBOOK

I hope your Christmas season is everything you want it to be and nothing you don't want it to be this year. If you have updates or photos of your Christmas to share, Tweet or post them to IG with hashtag #christmased and look at other people's posts at that hashtag.

Please send comments and suggestions for additions to the workbook to me at askmoxie@gmail.com or through Twitter to @AskMoxie

If you'd like to sign up for my not-at-all-regular free email with ideas about being yourself while you're being a parent (not parenting advice), go to AskMoxie.org and put your name in the signup box in the right-hand column.

ABOUT THE AUTHOR

"If you have come to help me, you are wasting your time; but if you are here because your liberation is bound up with mine, then let us work together." -- Lilla Watson

I'm Magda Pecsenye and I write AskMoxie.org, a website about being a parent and managing people, and working and being a parent.

I think parenting is the one thing that brings most of us to our knees. It's so important and so difficult-yet-simple that there's no way to ever feel like you're doing everything The Right Way. But I think most of us ARE doing it right on a minute-by-minute basis when we pay attention to ourselves and our kids and focus on maintaining a good relationship.

I think you already have everything in you that you need or will ever need to be a great parent. You are the best parent for your child.

I love Christmas and have always loved Christmas, but I've also been the loneliest I've ever been and felt like a complete fraud at Christmastime. I wrote this workbook because I wanted to work through it myself, so I thought you might, too.

Merry Christmas, and a Happy New Year!

Made in the USA
Middletown, DE
06 November 2015